ACING THE UNDERGRAD
YOUR PERSONAL MENTOR

ACING THE UNDERGRAD
YOUR PERSONAL MENTOR

Emeka V. Anazia & Carrie V. Anazia

authorHOUSE®

AuthorHouse™ LLC
1663 Liberty Drive
Bloomington, IN 47403
www.authorhouse.com
Phone: 1-800-839-8640

Published by AuthorHouse   08/21/2013

ISBN: 978-1-4918-1108-5 (sc)
ISBN: 978-1-4918-1107-8 (e)

Library of Congress Control Number: 2013915274

Contents

PREFACE

College! Can you believe what some call the most exciting years of your life have arrived? For many of you, it is the start of adulthood. You have the responsibility and power to shape your destiny. Let's be real. This is one of the most important chapters of your life, which directly impacts your future. Many people unfortunately don't realize this until it is too late, and inevitably waste their college experience.

We, Emeka and Carrie, both graduated from college Summa Cum Laude, were heavily involved with extracurricular activities (including holding leadership positions and mentorship roles), and worked part time jobs, while thoroughly enjoying every moment of our college lives. In this book, we will be your personal mentors and share with you college fundamentals, personal examples, and specific tips for achieving all that you can during your years of college. If you follow them, we guarantee it will help you accomplish your goals, get the most out of college, and ultimately ACE the undergrad!

Use this book by first selecting your mentor. We both have very different personalities, strengths, experiences, and work habits. We were able to ace the undergrad in our own unique ways. You can choose to read the book from the perspective of the mentor whose personality you identify with more. Or, you can choose both mentors to help you see differing perspectives on how to incorporate the same necessary skills into your college lives. When you have chosen your mentor, the chapters begin.

Each chapter gives you an overview of a specific skill, or college fundamental, that you must master in order to become a successful college student. Following the overviews, we help guide you through your college experience by providing concrete personal examples of how we actually came to mastering the skills, and how mastering them greatly impacted our college lives. Then, in the last part of every chapter, you will receive practical tips on how you can apply these skills to your college experience.

In our opinion, the vast majority of self-help books focus only on empowering and motivating the reader to achieve a particular goal. Yes, it is great to be encouraged, but that encouragement will always be short-lived if not supported by practical steps to reach the goal. We wanted to not only tell you what needs to be done, but also to explicitly demonstrate how it can be done. We believe in these ten college fundamentals wholeheartedly, as we have personally experienced the results of having used each of them. Also, we have seen what happens when students do not apply these important skills. We are convinced that if you read the entire book and follow our advice consistently, you too will be successful and ace the undergrad.

SELECT YOUR MENTOR

Emeka

Energetic
Big picture oriented
Straightforward
Idealistic
Prefers teamwork
Works well under pressure
Extrovert
Logic driven
Planner
Talkative
Confident

Carrie

Easy going
Detail oriented
Compassionate
Realistic
Prefers individual work
Prefers preparation time
Introvert
Emotion driven
Spontaneous
Competitive
Determined

CHAPTER 1
SET GOALS

What is Your Game Plan?

Before stepping foot onto your college campus, your personal goals must be established. Set goals in the beginning of your college career that are tailored to what you want to gain during your time in college. You might want to graduate with a 4.0 G.P.A., study abroad, play a competitive sport, run for a position in your school's Student Government Association, or acquire an internship before you graduate. Whatever your goals are, you need to set them and write them down. Post them in a place where you can always be reminded of them, so you will never lose focus of the target.

1

College holds an incredible amount of opportunities that are just waiting for students to reach out and grab. However, before you can take them, you have to know what it is that you truly want from college. Without knowing what you want, you may pass up amazing opportunities, without even realizing it. Having a college plan-of-action helps you to better understand what you want, and actually acquire those benefits that are best for your life. Do not come to college without a game plan. Many students who enter college without a game plan end up graduating without the diverse experiences that were available to them; or worse, they fail to graduate at all. Don't let this be you.

Realize that setting goals does not mean that your passions and desires cannot change. During our experiences in college, we found ourselves changing our goal lists by adding goals, revising them, and even choosing to continue some of our more challenging goals post college and into the working world. Simply put, setting goals gives you a plan and some direction as to where you want to be in the future. Having these goals helps you acquire clear vision and focus, which leads to success and greatness in your college career. Know what you want, and go get it.

Emeka

As a freshman, I established my personal goals at the beginning of the academic year. Someone once told me that having at least a 3.5 G.P.A. in college would open many doors for me in regards to internships and scholarships. Therefore, I made my first goal to graduate with at least a 3.6 G.P.A. My second goal was to obtain an internship before I graduated. I knew that this was a necessary goal for me so that I could gain work experience in my field of study, strengthen my skill set, and ultimately determine if the corporate world would be a good fit for my future career. My next goal was to acquire leadership positions on campus by holding offices in various organizations. I made this a goal because I wanted a way to meet people, build my leadership skills, and make a difference on my campus. In addition, my next goal was to find four potential partners to start a business. I am an entrepreneur at heart, and it had always been my dream to start a company. I knew I needed a team to make this dream a reality. My final goal, on a more personal note, was to find my wife in college. This goal was inspired by my frustration in watching television sitcoms showing people in their 30's still going to bars every week and living the "single life". I didn't want that for my life. I guess you can consider me a family man.

I created a very diverse list of goals, wrote them down, posted them on my dorm room wall, and immediately started taking steps toward pursuing each of them. By the end of my college experience, I graduated with a 3.8 G.P.A., acquired a co-op (a 6-month internship), held many campus leadership positions in SGA and other organizations, and found my wife. Having my goals to keep me focused led me to even overachieve on some of them. I didn't meet my goal of finding four potential business partners while at college; but this is a long-term goal that I am continuing to strive for after college. Having a game plan gave me clear vision to help me reach my full potential in college. That is the key. In looking for those business partners, I expanded my network greatly and met many amazing individuals who I still stay in touch with to this day. In diligently striving for your goals, you will gain valuable life experiences and obtain unforeseen benefits from your efforts.

Carrie

When I first entered college, I made a "bucket list," which was a listing of all the endeavors I wanted to pursue and accomplish before I graduated from college. I purposefully made my bucket list as ambitious as possible to take advantage of all that college had to offer. My main goal was to graduate with a perfect 4.0 G.P.A. I chose this because I knew that someone had to be valedictorian of my graduating class, and I asked myself, "Why couldn't this person be me?" Since I couldn't provide a legitimate answer to this question, I made it my number one goal. My other personal goals were to study abroad, meet as many people as I could, and get accepted into an Ivy League graduate school. Creating these goals gave me focus and determination to make sure that they were accomplished before I completed my four years of undergrad. I even told my goals to a mentor at my college. She reminded me of my goals and inquired about the progress I was making toward them after every semester, which added an extra layer of accountability on my part. I was able to accomplish all of my goals and a few more that I developed along the way because I started from day one with writing them down and planning accordingly for success.

Tips

1. Create your goals by asking yourself why you are going to college and what you want to accomplish in college.

2. Make your goals ambitious. Don't settle for mediocrity.

3. Write down your goals. They can be easily forgotten.

4. Post your goals in a clearly visible spot as a daily reminder.

5. Review your progress toward your goals after each semester.

6. If you fail at a goal, don't give up. Revise the goal and start where you left off.

7. Tell your goals to a person you trust to increase your accountability.

Extra: Some Generic Goals Everyone Should Have:

1. Graduate in four years with a 3.5 G.P.A. or higher.

2. Join a school club, sport, or organization.

3. Hold a leadership position.

4. Acquire an internship in your field.

5. Live on campus for at least one year.

6. Meet as many people as you can.

7. Work out at least once a week.

CHAPTER 2
TIME MANAGEMENT

Where Did the Time Go?

With so many things to do, places to go, and people to see, college can leave you asking yourself, "Where did all the time go?" As a college student, you will have to attend classes, dine in the cafeteria, convene for group assignments, complete homework, study, and meet with professors . . . just to name a few. Let's also not forget about meeting new people, going to parties, and exploring! The socializing aspect of college is great as long as it doesn't become a distraction for you. The only way to truly achieve a balance is to be a master of time management.

Your college days will inevitably be filled with a variety of tasks. You might ask, "What types of things can be considered a college task?" Well, it's very simple. Your tasks are anything and everything that occupy your time in the day. These can include anything from homework assignments to social events. Effective time management means to be aware of your tasks that need to be completed, and to finish those tasks on time, in order of importance. In order to master your time management, it is necessary to have an effective and efficient way of organizing and prioritizing your tasks. We suggest that you develop a method of recording all of your tasks together, so you can visualize all of your upcoming duties. Some people write down their tasks in a planner, on a calendar, or input them into their smart phones. Whatever you decide to do, make sure it is easy and convenient to access. This will help you to organize your days by correctly allocating your time to make sure that everything you plan to do actually gets completed by its deadline.

Hopefully, one of your goals in college is to not only graduate, but to graduate with excellence and achieve a 3.5 G.P.A. or higher. Students who do not use their time effectively will not be able to achieve this goal. Without time management skills, students often forget specific obligations, turn in assignments late, miss meetings, suffer from procrastination, turn in below average work, earn poor grades, feel overwhelmed, and become stressed. Without a strong ability to manage your time, you will never be able to fully enjoy your college experience while maximizing your productivity, and becoming the superstar you want to become. Performing well in college will open many doors for you, but can only be accomplished by having excellent time management skills. Remember, time is valuable and you can't get it back. Don't waste your time in college.

Emeka

Have you ever heard of the saying, "out of sight, out of mind"? Simply put, if you do not see something regularly, you will forget about it. That phrase could not be any truer for me. In order for me to be aware of something, it needs to be easy to see and easy to access. This area for me was my planner. I utilized great time management by writing down all my tasks in this planner. I wrote down when I needed to study, send an email, clean my room, or even visit a friend. I didn't care how significant or trivial my tasks seemed. If it needed to be done, I needed to write it down.

Next, I would draw a small box beside each individual task written in my planner. The boxes were my indicator of which tasks still needed to be completed. I would check each box when its corresponding task was accomplished. This gave me a visual of how many tasks I had completed and had left to complete during the day. I could also glance at the week as a whole to determine if it would be a "heavy week" or a "light week," depending on the amount of tasks I had written down, and how long I presumed they would take to complete. How I would go about my day was contingent upon the quantity and length of tasks I had left. For example, if I had numerous tasks left, then I would have to turn down requests to "hang out." Another way I managed my time was with my cell phone. I used my cell phone as an alarm clock and calendar to alert me as to when various activities were starting, approaching, or ending. I kept both my planner and my cell phone with me most of the time.

We are all human. Sometimes duties slip our minds. These time-management techniques helped me to become a person of excellence. They helped me to be a punctual person, who was committed to his word. It is important to develop a method that works for you and to stick to it.

Carrie

In college, you have to be a "planner." You have too many responsibilities to keep up with to be a "winger." I found out in college that it is important to plan for the long term (the semester) and for the short term (day by day). My long term planning consisted of writing down everything in my planner, from due dates on assignments, to group meetings, to on-campus events. At the beginning of each semester, I would acquire a syllabus in all of my classes that contained a class calendar of assignment due dates for the semester. Once I had these, I transferred all of my assignments and their due dates into my planner for the entire semester. Sometimes, since I can be very detail-oriented, I would even color code my assignments by which class they were assigned. I would cross each assignment off when it was completed. Yes, I was a little obsessive, but it worked for me.

Since I used my planner as my main way of managing my tasks, the assignments from all of my classes were not separated and unorganized in various places. With my method, I could see everything that I had to accomplish altogether in one planner that I transported almost everywhere. Using this technique gave me a clear visual of my semester, which allowed me to best determine how to pace myself.

My short term planning consisted of a simple weekly outline. I posted this outline on the wall in my dorm room because it was my weekly structure. It included all the tasks that remained constant during the semester. I could see the entire week at a glance, which illustrated my class times, when I would make it to the cafeteria, when I would exercise, weekly club meetings, etc. This outline gave me stability in a college world that was constantly demanding my precious time. When anything new came up, like an event on campus that I wanted to attend, I would evaluate my schedule and decide whether to work it in or to decline. You will have time in college to accomplish all that you need to, but you just have to figure out how to use time wisely. My short term and long term planning methods helped me minimize the procrastination and stress that college is capable of imposing.

Tips

1. Remember, you can't major in partying. Prioritize your tasks so that academics come first.

2. Write down all of your assignments, even the small things, and check them off when completed.

3. Locate class assignments from your professors' syllabi and write them down.

4. Reward yourself after completing an assignment (i.e. 30 min break).

5. While completing an assignment, turn off all distractions (i.e. social networking) so you can take full advantage of the time you have allotted for the task.

6. Take advantage of holidays. Have fun, but set some time aside to get ahead on your personal goals (i.e. school work, applying for scholarships, etc.).

7. The weekend is not a vacation. During your college years, it is understood that you will have homework and studying to complete over the weekend.

8. Obtain a copy of the curriculum guide for your major and stick to it. You don't want to stay in college longer than needed because you accidentally took courses that didn't count toward your graduation requirements.

CHAPTER 3
HOW TO SUCCEED
IN CLASS

Got Classroom Etiquette?

In order to succeed in your classes, you need to be aware of three things: completing homework, studying daily, and demonstrating respect to your professors. These tips seem simple, but you will quickly realize how many people don't utilize good classroom etiquette. Without letting these three important concepts become ingrained in your life, success will never be a standard for you.

Most people are aware of the first concept, homework. Any assignment that your professor expects you to complete outside of the classroom is considered homework. Examples of college homework assignments include written papers, assigned readings, questions from a textbook, or the preparation of class presentations. It is important to not only turn in your homework, but to turn in high quality work by the time it is due. In college, you are given ample time to complete your homework. Refer to your syllabus and start early on your assignments. Keep in mind that there is no penalty for turning assignments in early. Some teachers will even allow you to turn in assignments early and give you feedback before you submit the final draft by the designated due date.

To master the art of doing homework, you must be a person willing to go the extra mile. Before turning in written papers, have someone proofread them. Or, if writing is not your strength, make a trip to the writing center on your campus to get help. For assigned reading articles or book chapters, most people will skim through the material just to get it over with or fail to read it at all. However, we advise that you read them closely. Underline, highlight, or make notes of important points. You will be expected to participate in class, and not having read could impact your grade. Lastly, in preparing classroom presentations, ask for a rubric from your professor, and make sure to include all the necessary parts. Then, use your creativity to design a presentation that will keep your audience's attention. Invite in a guest speaker, perform a skit, create a survey, etc. There is nothing worse than experiencing a person with a monotone voice, reading a PowerPoint presentation filled with plain text, who fails to make eye contact with the audience. Take your homework seriously.

The next concept is studying. There is a broad misconception that homework and studying are the same. This is far from the truth. Yes, homework and studying have their similarities. They are both completed outside of normal class hours, and they both are necessary to your success. However, homework is externally assigned, while studying is internally assigned. Studying is your personal effort to acquire knowledge and further your understanding. A person can show study habits by taking the time to review notes after class, reread chapters, create outlines, and complete practice problems. Remember that studying is not something that should only be attempted the day before an exam. This is called cramming, and is ineffective. Take time to study after class in preparation for the next class session, so you can truly learn the material. When you study, make sure distractions are kept to a minimum. You can also increase your focus and motivation by going to a library or study room to surround yourself with other people who are working hard.

You might ask, "How do you know when you have studied enough?" You have studied enough when you have a strong command of the material learned and can clearly explain it to others. There is no set time on studying because everyone is different. We all have our different strengths in this world. Some people grasp concepts quicker than others. If you are a person who needs more time to process academic material, then do what you need to do. Remember, that your G.P.A. is not an indicator of how smart you are. It is an indicator of how hard you work. If you truly want to ace the undergrad, completing homework alone will not cut it. You have to have strong study habits.

The last concept is the respect factor. Respecting your professors is the little known variable that can either make your college experience extremely successful or utterly disastrous. Respecting your professors means that you do everything in your power to show your professors that you take their classes seriously. You show them that you value and appreciate their expertise. Also, you demonstrate that you believe that their class and the knowledge they are sharing is worth your time and will ultimately benefit you in life. If you genuinely believe these things, it will manifest in your actions in the classroom.

You can show respect by coming to class on time every class session, maintaining eye-contact when the teacher is speaking, thanking the professors for shedding light or providing clarity on a topic, or by contributing your thoughts, opinions, questions, and ideas to the learning environment. The respect factor is more than a skill that will get you far in college; it is a life skill. However, we have seen many students intentionally or unintentionally disrespect their professors. They have slept in class, sporadically attended class sessions, strolled into class late without any class materials, or have been verbally disruptive. There is a small chance that their professors had any mercy on these students when it came down to their grades. Respect is something you have to give in order to receive.

These three concepts should not be used in isolation. They must all be used together to the best of your ability. Keeping these three concepts in mind and putting them into practice daily in college will help you to achieve success in the classroom.

Emeka

Whenever I entered a classroom, I did my best to learn from and respect the professor. I showed up to class on time, turned in assignments by their deadlines, always asked thought-provoking genuine questions, and visited the professors during their office hours. I learned early in life that we are all equal as human beings, and everyone deserves to be treated the way you would like to be treated. That philosophy has carried me far in life with acquiring many friendly acquaintances, including some who are professors. Treat your professors with respect. It blew my mind when I would see students sleeping in class, disrupting the learning environment, and skipping classes. Oftentimes, I would notice these same students at the end of the semester begging for a good grade. This obviously will not get you very far in your college career. Don't be that student.

I always took my schoolwork very seriously. I did whatever it took to comprehend the material. I would read and reread designated chapters and review my notes until I understood the information to the point where I could teach someone else. If I didn't understand something, I would ask the professor or other students in the class for help. Don't be lazy, make excuses, and just give up. Do whatever is in your power to comprehend the material. If you are smart enough to get into college, then you are smart enough to grasp the knowledge. Don't be intimidated. You are just like everyone else who has gone through college before you. You can do it.

Carrie

I chose to always remember that there is a difference between doing homework and studying. I always made sure that my homework assignments were turned in on time. I analyzed my classes and realized that some classes require extensive studying. In classes like those, I would do just that . . . study. Math was never my strong suit. I was the type of student in high school that would work my butt off for a C average in a math class. To my demise, I was informed that I had to take math classes in college, too. I, again, had to work extremely hard there and take advantage of every opportunity to receive help. I never just stopped at completing the assigned math homework problems. I knew that I needed extensive practice of the math skills everyday in order to be successful. I began completing online practice problems on my own. I also frequently asked my friend, who was a math education major, to teach me the more difficult concepts in a different way after class. With all of the extra math practice that I purposefully sought out, I had no choice but to earn an A.

Also, as I became an upper classman, my major classes became increasingly more demanding. After each class session, I would review the new material and make notes to prepare for the next class session, as if there would be a pop quiz when I entered. I chose to take each of my classes seriously, even the ones that others viewed as "easy" classes. This showed that I respected my professors and the knowledge they were providing me.

Other ways that I showed respect were by coming to class each day on time, prepared to learn, discuss, and contribute. The best way to be a respectful student is to monitor your thinking. You are not in college and going to class just for a grade. You are there to learn and grow as an individual. I came to class with a genuine care and curiosity about the material being presented. Being an education major, I wanted to learn so that I could become an amazing teacher after graduation. Always know that in your later career, you will need to apply the material and skills that you learned in college. Be a sponge and soak up as much knowledge as you can.

Tips

1. Homework—We all struggle with homework sometimes. If you are struggling, DON'T give up. There are many strategies you can use to get help. Check to see if your school has tutoring, ask classmates for help, or even check Google or YouTube.

2. Studying—Make sure when you study there are no distractions. Go to the library or a study room if your dorm room has too many distractions. Form study groups before tests so that you can learn from other students who have a strong mastery of the material.

3. Respect—Sit in the front row or the center of a classroom. Professors are people just like you. Treat them the way you would like to be treated no

matter the circumstance. That is what it means to be a person of integrity. Show interest in their class and get to know them during their office hours. Lastly, remember to ask questions. Professors love when students ask thought-provoking questions that show they are paying attention in class and are curious about the material.

CHAPTER 4
GET TO KNOW YOUR PROFESSORS

Professors, Friend or Foe?

An average college size is about 15,000 students. Wow! In an environment this large, it is extremely easy to blend into the crowd. It is awfully tempting to just show up to class, take notes, then leave, and never have to personally meet your professors. We don't care if you are sitting in a small class of twelve students, in an auditorium of 300 students, or alone in your dorm room taking an online course. Your professor should know you by more than just the grade they have in their grade book. They should know your career goals, your involvement at the university, and your dedication to their classroom. Also, you should know about their experiences, interests, and accomplishments. We learned while in college to never try to make it through undergrad as an island. You need people, especially your professors, to help you along your undergraduate career. They can greatly influence your academic progress.

Not only should you know your professors, but they should know you, too. You can ensure this by talking to them after class one-on-one, or by visiting them during their office hours. If they aren't very accessible, send them an email stating that you would like to meet with them briefly. Professors respect it when students take the initiative to visit them during their office hours. Stopping by to visit your professors will truly distinguish you from the average student. When you meet with your professors, you can ask them for clarity when you don't understand a topic or assignment. Also, if you and your professor share an interest, you can discuss their professional experiences. For example, if your major is nursing and your professor has been a nurse, take this great opportunity and get to know about their experiences. If you are unsure of what you want to pursue as a career, ask them for advice. There are many great conversation starters to help you build a relationship with your professors. You should never wait until the last week before final exams to get to know them. Never underestimate the power in professor-student relationships.

Building relationships with your professors can hold many benefits. Many professors have connections to companies that can lead to potential internship or job opportunities if they are aware of you. Also, your professors have the potential to provide excellent letters of recommendation or references for graduate school or potential jobs. Additionally, many scholarships require professors' nominations. If you are "in the know," you could be recommended. Lastly, your professors can serve as mentors for you, offering you valuable professional or personal advice. Professors will help you out as much as they can in their classroom, and beyond the classroom, when they feel connected to you and believe in you. They can be your strongest supporters in college and beyond.

Emeka

I understood very early in my college career that professors are regular people just like you and me, but with Ph.Ds. With that in mind I did my best to learn from them, share with them my goals and ambitions, and listen to their advice for my life. I built genuine relationships with my professors and am still friends with some of them today. Because of the rapport I built with my professors I was able to get amazing letters of recommendation, incredible job references, and I was fortunately connected to dozens of scholarships and business competitions. I acquired my first job out of college because of the help from a professor. Connect with your professors. They can be powerful allies in your network.

Benefits From Building Relationships:

- I won over $20,000 in scholarship money after enrollment at the university from the support of my professors writing letters of recommendation.

- I won two scholarships simply from my professors nominating me for the awards.

- My Academic Chairperson invited me to participate in a social business competition where my team competed against graduate school students from all across the state. Due to our efforts, our school surprised us with scholarship money.

- The Dean of my college invited me to the Ph.D. Project Conference, which was a fully paid trip to Chicago, where I learned what it takes to earn a Ph.D.

- One of my professors was connected to a director at my first perspective job. That relationship was an asset towards landing me the job.

- My relationship with the Honors Program administration at my college helped me to become hired by the Honors Program for two years as an Academic Success Coach.

Carrie

Whenever I had a question about an assignment or just needed more clarity, I stopped by my professor's office. This showed my professors that I was serious about my education. Sometimes I even stopped by their offices when I knew I was going to be in the building or have a few extra minutes to chat and update them on how I was doing. When your professors know you by name, your character, and your work ethic, they will help you succeed. Whenever I needed a letter of recommendation or academic support, my professors were more than happy to go the extra mile to help me. Many of them showed me that they would do anything in their power to make sure that I was successful.

After I graduated from undergrad and graduate school, I needed a reference from one of my professors for a highly competitive teaching position for which I had applied. There were two other candidates that were also in the running for the position. After we all had interviewed, the principal of the school still did not know which applicant to choose, as both of the other applicants had plenty of teaching experience, something that principals love to see on resumes. I was fresh out of college with absolutely no full-time teaching experience. The principal called me to let me know that he would be calling all of our references to get a clear depiction of who would be the best fit for the position. The next day, I got offered the job. The principal said that he was very impressed by the amazing accolades that my professor gave me. He stated that he was fascinated that she knew exactly who I was, was able to give detailed examples of my credentials and experiences while in college, and knew specifics about my goals, aspirations, work ethic and overall character. I got the job, not only from my hard work in college, but also because of the strong relationships that I built with my professors.

Tips

1. Visit your current and previous classroom professors and academic advisor periodically.

2. In addition to your professors, make sure you get to know and keep in touch with your department chairperson, dean, and administrative assistants.

3. Awareness is key. Administrators and professors that are aware of you will tell you about various academic and professional opportunities.

CHAPTER 5
GET INVOLVED

How Big is Your Network?

We are always surprised when we meet someone who isn't enjoying their college experience. Throughout our years, we've found something in common with all of them. None of them were involved with any activities on campus and had a very small network. We go to college to learn, but the college experience is so much more than just going to class and doing homework. To get the most out of your college experience, you have to get involved with activities on campus. There are many college clubs, organizations, and athletic teams on your campus that are looking for members and leaders. You can join an academic or departmental organization, an honor society, a special interest group, a student government association, a campus ministry, or even an intramural sport. There is literally something for everyone. There are karate clubs, marching bands, modeling troupes, or ROTC. Make sure you pick an organization or two and get involved.

You can find the types of involvement your school has to offer by organization fairs, campus involvement centers, website listings of clubs, or by word of mouth. It is a shame when students come to college and never get connected. They stay confined to their own small circle of friends and never open up to new friends. No matter what college you attend, there will be a plethora of people with different interests, backgrounds, talents, and experiences. Meet as many of them as you can. Evaluate your interests, find something to get involved in, and step outside your comfort zone. Once you have found something, decide if you want to push yourself even further and hold a leadership position in it. If you find that there is a need that your school does not have, start an organization for it. It's all about making an impact and improving your college community.

Becoming involved in your campus can truly enhance your college experience. Joining organizations is a great way to meet people and build your network. When you come to college, you leave your family and friends behind. Depending on how far your college is away from your home, you may rarely see them during your years in college. Because of this, you will be better off if you meet as many people as you can to build a community in your home away from home. Many of the friends you meet in college will continue to be your friends throughout life. Besides building your network, getting involved on campus helps you to enhance your resume. It communicates to your future employers that you were a person who went the extra mile in college. Additionally, being involved on campus helps you to become more connected to your school because of the role you have played in your organization. You end up enjoying your experience more because it gives your time at college more meaning.

Emeka

I love helping people and felt that being in the student government association at my school would give me more opportunities to do so. So, during my freshman year in college I decided to run for Freshman Class Vice-President. The odds were against me because I was an out-of-state student. I didn't already have a network of people that could help me or would vote for me because they already knew me, like the other candidates. I didn't let that stop me and took it as an opportunity to meet people. I prepared a small speech letting people know a little about myself and what I wanted to do to help my college. I took my speech and talked to students in the dorms across campus. People saw that I was genuine and supported me to win the office. Don't let anything stop you from striving for your goals or getting involved at school. Always try your best and meet as many people as you can.

In addition to SGA, I met people eating at the cafeteria, walking around campus, socializing at programs, playing basketball, etc. I genuinely liked meeting people and learning about their goals in life. I knew so many different people, that during a surprise birthday party that Carrie threw for me during my junior year, a guest, looking around at all of the party attendants, said, "Emeka sure has a diverse group of friends." It was funny at the time because it was so true. There were so many people in one room that were so different, they probably would have never interacted with each other on their own accord. It is just proof that I didn't discriminate and treated everyone with the same respect, no matter if they were a part of a certain organization or held a certain status. Get involved, and get to know your peers. This is key to having a great college experience.

Carrie

Just a few days into my freshman year of college, I met an upperclassman in the elevator of my dorm who told me to make sure that I meet as many people as I can in college. This was the most amazing advice that I received because doing so greatly enhanced the time I had at college and the love I had for my school and student body. During my freshman year, I immediately became a member of organizations such as the Honors program and Teaching Fellows. As I became an upperclassman, my campus involvement continued to grow, as I became a member of more clubs and honor societies, even holding offices in many of them. This was a great way to meet people and develop genuine relationships, while becoming heavily involved in planning multiple events for the benefit of my classmates and my community. In addition to being a part of multiple clubs and organizations on campus, I also made sure to attend events on campus weekly, such as athletic events, informative programs, and social gatherings. Balancing your academic life and your social life is essential to having an enjoyable and successful college experience.

Tips

1. Make sure going to the cafeteria and class are not the only times you leave your dorm room. Your college life will be so much better if you expand your boundaries. Trust us. There are so many different types of people in this world, and college is a melting pot for people with different interests. If you put yourself out there, you are bound to find friends to share your college experience.

2. It's easiest to meet people during your freshman year of college. You have the best ice-breaker in the world, which is that you are a freshman new to college. Ask other students about their major and what their goals are. From there, let the conversation flow.

3. Don't take Drake (the rapper's) advice about "no new friends." It is completely wrong. The more people you know, the more opportunities you have in life.

4. Remember college is supposed to be fun. If you are not having fun, get out and enjoy yourself! Just remember the tips from the earlier chapters.

Extra: Ice Breaker Questions

1. Where are you from?

2. Is this your first year in college?

3. What is your major?

4. Why did you choose this college?

5 What do you want to do with your major?

CHAPTER 6
BE A SUPERSTAR AND
SHINE WITH OTHERS

What's Your Tier?

If you stick to our tips you will meet plenty of people in college. That doesn't mean you should befriend everyone. Some people are fine being your acquaintances. Always remember that you want to surround yourself with people who have similar goals. It is much easier to stay motivated when you have friends who share your motivation. Your peers will help you stay on task with your homework, studying, and extra curricular activities as they work towards their own goals. College is more fun when you have peers by your side and you motivate each other to achieve excellence.

Having friends who aren't passionate about doing well in college and just want to have a "good time" may influence you in a negative manner. They may party too much and want you to come along. They might want you to engage in activities which will distract you from effective time management and completing your tasks. This type of distraction from your peers can ultimately make or break your college experience. We have seen it happen too many times.

Most things in life are comparable to a pyramid. The majority of people in college, as in life, are in tier one, represented by the bottom of the pyramid. These people occupy the largest part of the pyramid, and unfortunately, a large number of your college peers will fall into this category. These people want to get by with executing the bare minimum amount of effort possible. They spend most of their time partying and/or sleeping. Their professors have no clue who they are, or may only know them because of their bad classroom etiquette (chap. 3). Many times their grades drop so much that they lose their financial aid. They may or may not graduate on time or at all. Remaining in tier one and having the majority of your network consisting of tier one individuals will not get you very far in college.

Next, you will notice the students in the middle portion of the pyramid. This section is slightly smaller, because fewer of these students exist on college campuses. These are tier two students. They come to class most of the time and do what they are asked to do. However, they do nothing to set themselves apart from the norm and will most likely be considered average by future employers.

Lastly, there are college superstars. There will only be a small number of superstars on your campus and in your classes. These people represent the smallest portion at the top of the pyramid, the third tier. They do more than what is expected of them. They go over and beyond on all assignments, are extremely hard working, and are heavily involved on campus, while having their priorities in order. It is extremely likely that these students will have multiple job offers upon graduation. We encourage you to surround yourself with the superstars on your campus and to be one yourself.

Emeka

People who shared my passions and goals were a minority in college. Because of this, I had many acquaintances, but very few friends. I would "hang out" with many different groups of people, whether it was going to the cafeteria or going to their rooms. I would have fun with the positive aspects of the different groups. For example, with one group I'd play basketball, and with another, I'd have freestyle rap battles. The key is that I didn't let any person or group influence me negatively. If they were going to do something that didn't agree with my morals and values, I would not do it. I would explain to them my reasoning for choosing not to participate, and they would respect me. I have found that if you know who you are and stand by your convictions 100%, people will respect you, even if they don't agree with your reasoning. Focus on being a superstar and if you do it while helping others succeed, people will support you.

Carrie

In my college classes, there were few superstars. These were the types of people I liked having in my close friend circle. They were always easy for me to find, because they stood out and made an impression on their classmates and professors. All throughout college I completed homework and studied with them in study groups that we formed in the dormitory. Many times we planned to meet after class to complete assignments together and also teach each other difficult concepts. Working in study rooms can get long and tiring at times. For this reason, we often brought in food and music, and took breaks to just talk, which made studying a fun, social experience.

I also carried this mentality with me into graduate school. I surrounded myself with superstars there as well. They were students who would study with me, wake me up if I overslept, proofread my papers, and help me on projects. When it came time to spend hours studying for final exams, my group of superstars would actually agree to change each other's Facebook, Twitter, and Tumblr passwords so that we could not access these accounts and become distracted during those crucial days. Having the support of like-minded peers makes a world of a difference to your college success and overall experience. You need people around you who care and have a genuine concern for your academic and personal success. Having a group of people with similar goals and work ethic as me kept me motivated. We pushed each other to reach our full potential.

Tips:

1. Network with fellow superstars in each of your classes. Help each other with homework, projects, studying, and personal goals.

2. Don't spend too much of your college experience with tier one individuals.

3. Being a superstar will attract admirers, other superstars, and a few haters. Be humble toward your admirers, network with the other superstars, and ignore the haters.

CHAPTER 7
OPPORTUNITIES

Take It or Leave It?

In order to make the most out of your college experience, take advantage of every opportunity that presents itself to you as long as it does not distract you from your overall college goals. College opportunities can include things like: running for a leadership position, holding programs on campus, and speaking in front of large audiences. Other examples include studying abroad, participating in competitions, and attending conferences. Your time in college is your chance to explore all possibilities, take on new passions, and live up to your aspirations. Once you graduate from college and enter the working world, it is more difficult to have the time and guidance to explore, travel, and meet certain goals. There is nothing like the support you have in college.

If you follow our advice in this book, it is expected that many opportunities will come your way. Don't focus on what you might lose, and pass up opportunities. Taking on these challenges will only bring positive results to your life. For example, when you hear about an essay competition, you will notice that most people will choose not to participate. However, if you take the time to enter the competition and complete your essay to the best of your ability by its due date, you will have a strong chance at winning possible scholarship money. Also, in the event that you do not win, the experience within itself will improve your writing skills and expand your network. No matter what the opportunity may be, there are many benefits that can be gained by simply not passing it up. This is how you must view life. Look at every opportunity as a blessing that will make you a better person.

We understand that with each new opportunity there is a possibility of it bringing a degree of fear. However, you must remember that preparation destroys fear. Imagine all of the people you admire in this world who may be incredible public speakers, great athletes, professional entertainers, or entrepreneurs. Realize that they had to practice and prepare for their tasks. Michael Jackson did not just enter a concert stage and perform. He practiced numerous times before any event! Don't let fear be an excuse for not taking advantage of an opportunity. With preparation in a timely manner, you can do many great things.

Emeka

I had many opportunities presented to me while in college. Some of them allowed me preparation time, while others put me on the spot. No matter the opportunity, when it came to being in front of an audience, I was fearful. On the occasions in which I ran for Freshman Class Vice President and Junior Class President, I had to give a speech in front of about 200 students. In a different year, I was asked to present for a social business competition in front of 400 people. And another time, at the last minute, I was asked to be the Master of Ceremony for the annual honors banquet, where I spoke in front of about 300 people. For each event, I was terrified. But, I believed in my abilities and knew that if I prepared, I could do it. For each new opportunity, I took as much time as was available to prepare and practice what I wanted to say until I knew my part inside and out. People were pleased with my speeches and each opportunity brought new benefits into my life.

Opportunities Taken and Benefits Received:

1. From running for Freshman Class VP and Junior Class President, I gained public speaking experience, served as an SGA officer, enhanced my resume, and greatly expanded my network.

2. From participating in the Social Business Competition, I further developed my research skills, public speaking skills, and teamwork skills. I also won some scholarship money and networked with some amazing people.

3. From being the Master of Ceremonies at the Annual Honor's Banquet, I gained more public speaking experience and developed a greater relationship with the Honor's program administration. Due to this experience, the Honor's Program administration became more aware of my work ethic and helped me acquire jobs within the Honor's Program for the next two years.

Carrie

In college, I did my best to take advantage of every opportunity available. I tried not to pass up opportunities that I knew would help me to grow as a person, even if it required that I step outside of my comfort zone. What I would tell myself is that feeling uncomfortable means you are growing. Many times, I would hear about various opportunities for students via email or word of mouth. I knew I wanted to make the most out of my college years; therefore, I was constantly signing up to take on these new challenges. Every time I heard that my college was taking students on a trip to a different country, I always signed up to go. Because of this, I studied abroad three different times in various countries around the world.

My first study abroad trip was my sophomore year. I went to Ghana, West Africa. This was a trip that completely took me out of my comfort zone. I spent over a week in a foreign country without the ability to call home, I could not speak or understand the different languages of the various tribes, and I lived with a host family in a village without running water and little electricity. However, while I was there, I engaged in community service activities at a nearby village school, taught some middle schoolers about American culture, and learned a ton about Ghanaian culture. I still stay in touch with some of the amazing people I met in Ghana. I even have had my students that I currently teach to write pen pal letters to the students I met in Ghana. If I would have been frightened, and passed up this trip, I would have never reaped the great once in a lifetime opportunities that I experienced. College is an amazing time to explore and to try things you have never tried before. Do all you can. Don't hold back.

Tips:

1. Following our advice in this book will bring many opportunities in your direction. Don't pass them up.

2. You can also find opportunities by looking at flyers around your campus, checking your school email and your school's website, and by asking your professors and advisors.

3. Each opportunity, no matter the outcome, will bring benefits to your life and help you develop into a better person.

4. Remember to prepare. Preparation is the key to your success.

CHAPTER 8
INTERNSHIPS

Want Experience?

Acquiring internships is crucial during your time in college. Internships are opportunities offered by companies to college students to work for their corporation, with a focus on training. Internships are offered for a fixed period of time, usually lasting for either a summer or for a semester (also known as a co-op). Whether paid or unpaid, internships provide college students valuable and practical experience in their field of study.

It is important to acquire an internship before you graduate because the working world is very different from the classroom. Internships allow you the opportunity to see how the skills you have learned in the classroom can be applied in a "real world" setting. They give you a better understanding of the big picture of what you are learning from your college professors. Also, when you are an intern, the company views you as a potential employee. Giving your best effort and doing an amazing job can ultimately lead to a future career with the company.

Additionally, if you do not choose to work for the company with which you completed your internship, other employers view your internship as relevant work experience. They see you as a candidate who took the initiative to "get their feet wet" in their field of study. Other benefits of acquiring internships include gaining insight into the type of career you would like to pursue, while expanding your network.

The best way to obtain an internship is by attending career fairs at your college or neighboring colleges. Career fairs give you the chance to meet with various companies' human resource employees face-to-face. It is a great way to personally connect with the company. Don't take career fairs for granted. Prepare for the career fairs by researching the companies you are interested in and by practicing your interview skills. Once you enter the career fair make sure you are dressed in business professional attire and have multiple resumes on hand. Most internships require at least a 3.0 GPA, professional references, an impressive resume, and a strong interview. It may seem like a lot, but it will come with ease as you strive to be a superstar.

Emeka

During my undergraduate experience, I participated in a co-op, which is a 6-month internship, with a Fortune 500 company. I became aware of the company from a friend who acquired the co-op the previous semester. She used her connections and put in a good word about me for the company. I was interested in interning with the company, so I researched the corporation and spoke with them at my college's career fair. They later scheduled an interview with me, and I was subsequently offered the co-op. In order to accept the co-op, I had to take one semester off of school. It was well worth it. It was an opportunity that gave me more awareness of what I wanted to do for my career.

The Details of How I Got This Co-op:

- My friend recommended me for the job (Chap. 5 & 6).

- The human resources representative from the company conducted a background check by asking professors and administrators about my character and work ethic (Chap. 4).

- I impressed the human resources representatives during the interview with my credentials (Chap. 1, 2, 3, 5).

Carrie

As an education major, internships are mostly built into our courses during our enrollment in college. I made sure to take all of my internships seriously and treat them as prolonged interviews for possible teaching positions in the future. During my internships in various elementary schools, I attempted to build strong relationships with the other workers and become a superstar on the job. I tried to view each internship as not just a course requirement to be completed, but instead view it as valuable field experience to get stronger in my teaching abilities.

In addition to these internships during the semesters, I never let my summer breaks go to waste while in college. During the summers, remember that you are still a college student, so this is a good time to pull your goals back out, review your progress toward them, and make necessary steps toward reaching them. Each summer, instead of enrolling in summer school, I engaged in a different endeavor that focused on my college goals. I chose to gain experience in working with students by acquiring tutoring or mentoring positions during my summers. I also had the opportunity to work closely with one of the professors of my college, conducting research, and ultimately got to present alongside her at a state conference for educators. None of these experiences were paid; however, they boosted my resume and helped me develop into the person I am today.

Tips

1. Companies look for potential interns by asking the college's administrators and previous interns for students who they think would be a good fit. Expanding your network in college will open doors for you for internships and other professional opportunities.

2. All of our jobs in life have been from recommendations. By doing your best in life and helping others, you will be noticed by people who will be willing to help you.

3. Prepare for career fairs at your college or neighboring colleges. Look up the companies that will be attending, and research the ones that interest you. Dress professionally, tell the companies what you like about them, and explain that you are interested in their internship opportunities.

4. Treat each internship as a prolonged interview process. That is what they are. The company is looking to determine if you are a good fit for them. Also, you should evaluate the company's culture and determine if it is a good fit for you.

CHAPTER 9
SCHOLARSHIPS AND
MONEY MANAGEMENT

Need Money?

Do you need money? Yeah, we all do. It is crucial that during your college years you manage your money well. Many people fall into heavy debt in college because they lack financial management skills. One simple way to avoid this is to only buy what you need. We never understood why people wanted to be so flashy in college. Materialistic things don't prove your worth in this world. Many of our friends spent their money at clubs/bars every weekend and on purchasing clothes while struggling to pay their rent. Make smart decisions. If you need financial literacy help, purchase a book that gives financial advice.

One source of money during your college years is the scholarship. Scholarships are free money that you should aggressively search and apply for. There are two types of scholarships which are merit-based and financial need-based. Merit scholarships are based on your academic credentials, and financial need scholarships are based on your family's income level. Keep in mind that all scholarships, whether merit or financial, may have other specific qualifications. Examples of qualifications are that you must have a certain major, be a minority, go to a certain school, live in a certain state, or be a certain classification.

The best way to search for scholarships is to search qualifications that you have on the internet. For example, if you are a female accounting major, search "accounting scholarships for women" in a search engine. Other ways to search for scholarships are to look for postings around your school, ask administrators, and check your school email. Even if you don't fit the income level for a financial need based scholarship that you find, we suggest that you still apply. You never know what can happen.

Emeka

I won many scholarships while in undergrad. I was fortunate to win over $10,000 in scholarship money in my final semester alone. I believe that if you follow our advice, you can win scholarship money, too. I had credentials and a story that people wanted to support (explained in chap.10). Are you somebody who helps make this world a better place and that people believe in? Give people something to believe in and they will support you.

Scholarships generally ask you to fill out an application form, write an essay, submit letters of recommendation, and submit a transcript by a deadline. As I wrote essays for various scholarships, I saved them and used them as a starting point, or template, for future scholarship essays. I gave my professors enough time to write a letter of recommendation before the due date—a one week minimum. My point is that scholarship applications get easier the more you do them. The process becomes repetitive and sometimes questions asked are very similar. I became a "pro" at applying for scholarships and you will, too.

With the money I acquired from scholarships and refund checks, I made sure all of my bills besides my tuition loans were paid off. I mainly used my money for food. Guys, it is simple. Only buy what you need. College is not a time to impress people with money you truly don't have.

Carrie

I was fortunate to attend undergrad with a full scholarship that I won my senior year of high school. I also received a $700 refund check every semester. I made sure to use that refund check explicitly on books and materials for my classroom success. Everything that was left, I saved. I bought as many used books as I could. I also did extensive research online to find the least expensive books. Never, ever buy all new books if you can help it. Purchasing books used costs much less than purchasing them new, which can help you save hundreds of dollars in the long run. At the end of the semester, I sold the books that I did not find useful to keep.

Also, the entire time I was in college, I acquired some type of income through working. I always held some type of part-time job. Most of the time, they were tutoring positions on campus, which were very convenient. This helped me to have money to enjoy myself, after all of my expenses were paid.

Additionally, while in college, I joined many organizations, clubs, and honor societies. Joining too many of these can become very expensive when it comes to membership fees. However, being a member of various honor societies offers scholarship opportunities and various discounts. I researched the honor societies that I was a member of and applied to all of the scholarships that I was eligible for. Some of them required that the supervisor of the organization only nominate one person from the chapter. Here is when building relationships with your professors comes into play again (Chap. 3, 4, & 5). I was fortunate enough to have been nominated on several occasions, and was able to win two major scholarships over all. One of those scholarships paid for a portion of my graduate school tuition.

Tips

1. Refund checks are disbursed after your financial aid has been applied. If you receive one, don't

blow it on a car, clothes, or the nightlife. Make sure your bills, such as rent, are paid off first.

2. Ask your professors and administrators about potential scholarships.

3. Buy a financial management book and apply its concepts.

Extra: Tips for saving money when buying textbooks

1. Check to see if you can use the previous edition of the required textbook for your class.

2. Rent your textbooks, whenever possible (chegg.com, bookstores, other students, etc.).

3. If you need to buy a textbook, check online for the least expensive one, then sell it back to your bookstore or online sites.

4. Check with others students who have previously taken the course to see if you can borrow their book for free for the semester.

5. Some books you may want to keep for your career. Buy them used, and hold on to them for future reference.

CHAPTER 10
THERE ARE NO EXCUSES

What's Holding You Back?

At the end of the day it is up to you for whether or not you want to be successful in college. We all have our struggles and burdens to bear in life. The challenge is to refrain from making excuses, but to focus on overcoming your burdens! The great thing is that once you overcome your struggles in life, you can use them as testimonies to help others and to help yourself. Our struggles help us build our character and give us an amazing/inspirational story to tell. Don't be ashamed of your struggles. Overcome them and use them to your advantage.

Emeka

One of my life's most profound setbacks occurred when I was in the eighth grade. A disease called Lupus attacked my kidney and almost killed me. I had multiple seizures, a massive stroke, was sent into a coma, and even lost all of my memory. I overcame this great hurdle and learned not to take life for granted. I had to work twice as hard as the average student to keep up in high school while my brain healed. Memorizing and quick comprehension continued to be a great problem for me. The lingering effect that the stroke had on me is that short-term memorization was not easy at all. During my college experience I had to develop techniques to help me memorize better. I personally wrote things down, read things out loud, created acronyms to master new concepts, and compared new topics with old topics I already knew. These tactics helped knowledge stick in my brain better. Doing these things took extremely hard work as I had to do them more than the average person. Instead of feeling embarrassed, ashamed, or defeated, I was constantly looking for ways to overcome my struggle. I frequently told my story to encourage other people and to explain who I was in interviews, speeches, and scholarship essays, which ended up helping me. Everyone has some type of burden or struggle in life, whether it is poverty, sickness, or family circumstance. Are you letting your weakness hold you back, or are you using it as a strength?

Carrie

All throughout life I struggled with a speech impediment. Grade school was a hard time for me as I struggled in areas of low self-esteem, humiliation, and withdrawal. My stuttering was extremely frustrating for me as I felt that I would never be able to clearly express myself. However, during college, my boyfriend at the time (now husband, Emeka) helped me to realize that I have the power to turn every one of my weaknesses into strengths. I learned to accept myself, imperfections and all, and use my burdens to be a blessing on other people. Now, I am comfortable enough with my stutter to write about it, hoping that my story will impact others. I even wrote about it on my graduate school personal statement, not for sympathy, but to give admissions a true understanding of who I was and my character in overcoming a major life obstacle. This helped me get accepted into each top-ranked graduate program that I applied to (Columbia, Harvard, and Vanderbilt). I have also used my story to help others in my teaching career. After getting to know my students, I understand that everyone has a story or burden to overcome. Some even have struggles with speech as I did. It does not matter what the story is, I use my burden to help my students and to show them how to turn their obstacles into opportunities. Any limitations people have in their lives should not control or defeat them. Once people unconditionally accept themselves, they can use their strengths to reach their full potential in life.

Tips

1.   Excuses are signs of the weak. Overcome your challenges in life; everyone has them.

2. Beating your challenges takes hard work, dedication, and perseverance. Some obstacles in life may seem extremely difficult, but anything's possible.

3. Overcome your struggles and then use them to your advantage. You can tell your story during interviews, scholarship essays, speeches, or simply to inspire others.

FINAL REMARKS

The advice in this book will help you to not only become successful in college, but also in life. It comes down to being a person of integrity. Be a person of your word and stay true to your commitments. If you do this you will go far in life, have successes, and be a person of greatness. Remember this, your college G.P.A. is not a reflection of your intellectual abilities; it is a reflection of the amount of effort and hard work put into your college experience. Good luck to you in your endeavors and remember to always do your best as you strive toward acing the undergrad!

MEET THE AUTHORS

Emeka V. Anazia

Emeka Anazia was born June 2, 1990 in Battle Creek, Michigan. He was raised in Columbus Ohio, and he also spent six years living in Topeka, Kansas. In 2008, Emeka was accepted into North Carolina A&T State

University's School of Business and Economics. As an honor student, Emeka maintained a 3.8 G.P.A. while being heavily involved in extracurricular activities and having a job. His leadership positions included Freshman Class Vice President, Alpha Lambda Delta chapter Vice President, Junior Class President, and American Marketing Association chapter President. He held mentorship jobs during all of his college semesters. He is a member of multiple honor societies, which include Alpha Lambda Delta, Golden Key, and Phi Kappa Phi. He also studied abroad in Singapore & Malaysia.

In 2012, Emeka graduated from North Carolina A&T summa cum laude, with a B.S. Degree in Supply Chain Management with over $20,000 in scholarship money won after enrollment. Now Emeka lives in Winston Salem, NC as a corporate employee, author, and real estate investor. He continues to learn and push toward achieving his goals.

Carrie V. Anazia

Carrie Anazia was born November 7, 1988 in Winston Salem, North Carolina. In 2007, she was accepted into North Carolina A&T State University's School of Education as an honor student, with a full $26,000 scholarship as a North Carolina Teaching Fellow. While in college, Carrie held leadership positions in several organizations each year, such as Kappa Delta Pi Honor society chapter secretary, Council for Exceptional Children chapter treasurer, and Alpha Lambda Delta Honor Society chapter community service coordinator. Carrie was also the creator and editor of *The Educator's Guild*, a newsletter about A&T Teaching Fellows.

Carrie also was able to study abroad on three different occasions while in college. She studied W.E.B. DuBois in Ghana, West Africa, studied business in Singapore and Malaysia, and studied the arts in France and Italy. In addition to making excellent grades, Carrie always found time for tutoring and mentoring opportunities during all four years of college with organizations such as AmeriCorps, Upward Bound, and Junior Achievement.

In 2011, Carrie graduated from A&T with a 4.0 G.P.A. as valedictorian, with a B.S. degree in Elementary Education and Special Education. Carrie then earned her Master's degree in Curriculum and Teaching: Elementary Education at Columbia University's Teacher's College in the city of New York. Carrie is currently teaching Exceptional Children in Winston Salem, NC.